EBOLA

HOW A VIRAL FEVER CHANGED HISTORY

by Mark L. Lewis

raintree

a Capstone company — publishers for children

Raintree is an imprint of Capstone Global Library Limited, a company incorporated in England and Wales having its registered office at 264 Banbury Road, Oxford, OX2 7DY – Registered company number: 6695582

www.raintree.co.uk
myorders@raintree.co.uk

Text © Capstone Global Library Limited 2020
The moral rights of the proprietor have been asserted.

Edited by Megan Ellis
Designed by Craig Hinton
Original illustrations © Capstone Global Library Limited 2020
Production by Katy LaVigne
Originated by Capstone Global Library Ltd
Printed and bound in India

978 1 4747 9087 1 (hardback)
978 1 4747 9091 8 (paperback)

British Library Cataloguing in Publication Data
A full catalogue record for this book is available from the British Library.

Acknowledgements
We would like to thank the following for permission to reproduce photographs: AP Images: ChinaTopix, cover (bottom), Diana Quintela/Global Images/Global Media Group/Sipa, 23, Sam Mednick, 29; Centers for Disease Control and Prevention: Aaron Sussell, Ph.D., M.P.H./Teresa Roebuck/Public Health Image Library, 19, Chief Petty Officer Jerrold Diederich/US Army Africa/Public Health Image Library, 27, Cleopatra Adedeji, RRT, BSRT/Public Health Image Library, 18, Frederick A. Murphy/Public Health Image Library, 10, Joel G. Breman, M.D., D.T.P.H./Dr. Lyle Conrad/Public Health Image Library, 13, National Institute of Allergy and Infectious Diseases (NIAID)/Public Health Image Library, 6, Sally Ezra/Public Health Image Library, 8–9; Getty Images: Olivier Douliery/White House Pool/ISP Pool Images/Corbis/VCG/Corbis News, 24; iStockphoto: gevende, 21, zeljkosantrac, 11; Red Line Editorial: 17; Shutterstock Images: Alexey Godzenko, cover (top left), Davide Calabresi, 5, jaddingt, cover (top right), Sergey Uryadnikov, 14–15, XiXinXing, 6–7. Design elements: Shutterstock Images.

CONTENTS

WORLDWIDE PANIC

Thomas Duncan travelled to the United States from Liberia. He wanted to visit his family. They lived in Texas.

Duncan felt sick after he arrived in Texas. He had a high fever and diarrhoea. Duncan went to the hospital on 26 September 2014. The doctor ordered tests to find out what was wrong. Nurses wrote a note saying Duncan had just arrived from Liberia. But the doctor did not see the note. The doctor sent Duncan home with antibiotics.

FAST FACT

The Centers for Disease Control and Prevention (CDC) thought as many as 1.4 million people might get Ebola in 2014. However, fewer than 30,000 people got the illness.

Duncan came back to the hospital on 28 September. He still had a fever and diarrhoea. This time the doctor saw the note. He worried that Duncan had something **contagious**. The doctor **isolated** Duncan on the hospital ward.

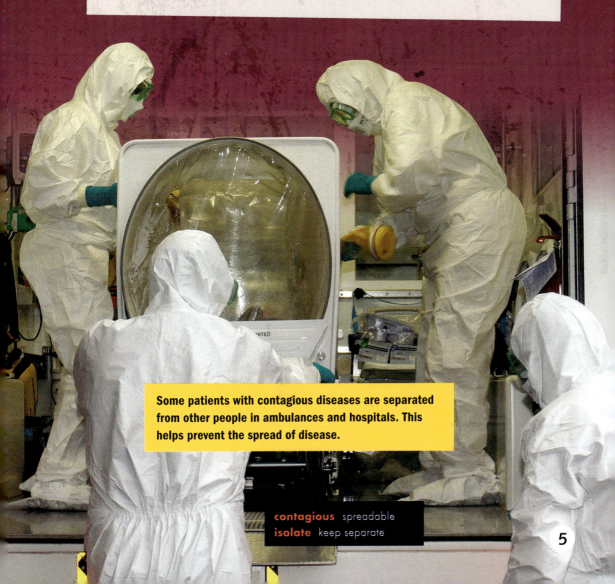

Some patients with contagious diseases are separated from other people in ambulances and hospitals. This helps prevent the spread of disease.

contagious spreadable
isolate keep separate

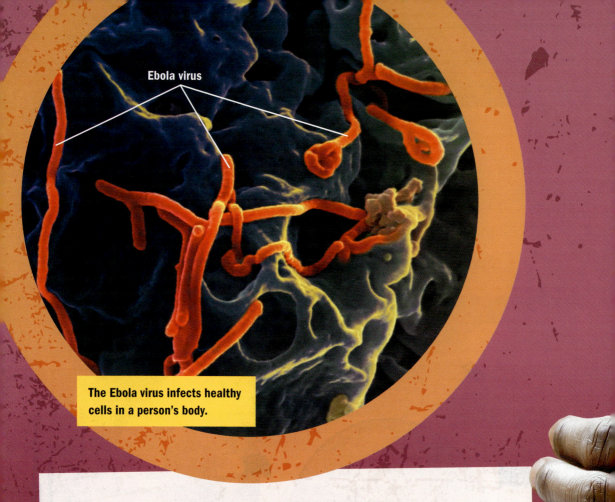

Ebola virus

The Ebola virus infects healthy cells in a person's body.

On 30 September, the test results came back. Duncan had Ebola. This was the first diagnosed case of Ebola in the United States.

TREATING DUNCAN

Ebola is a highly contagious virus. It is also deadly. Hospital workers had to be careful. Doctors wore special suits when visiting Duncan. Their skin was completely covered. The hospital room was cleaned with bleach.

Duncan was not getting better. He still had a fever. Doctors put him on **intravenous** (IV) fluids. He was **dehydrated**. Duncan could not eat. He could not get out of bed.

Doctors tried everything to cure Duncan. They even considered an **antiviral** medication. It was experimental. But Duncan died a week later.

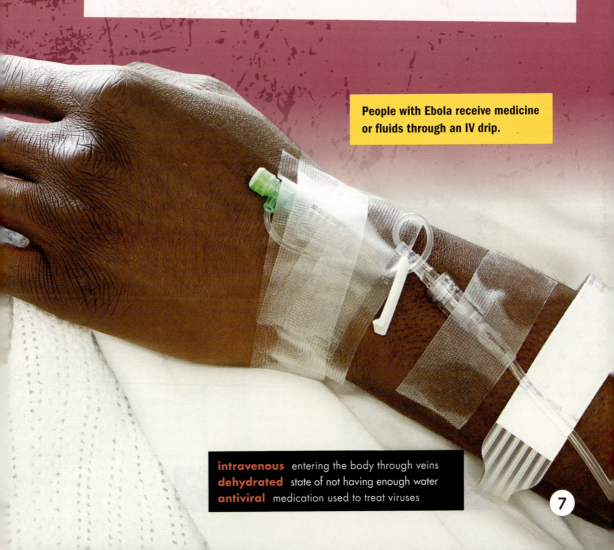

People with Ebola receive medicine or fluids through an IV drip.

intravenous entering the body through veins
dehydrated state of not having enough water
antiviral medication used to treat viruses

A GLOBAL DISEASE

There was an Ebola outbreak in Liberia in 2014. Government officials there tried to contain the virus. They wanted to stop it from spreading.

Duncan had been near people who had Ebola. Health workers tested Duncan when he arrived at the airport. Duncan did not show signs of illness. He did not have a fever. But Ebola has an **incubation period** of up to 21 days. Duncan did not know he was ill when he got on the plane.

FAST FACT

The United States sent 3,000 soldiers to help build hospitals for Ebola patients in Liberia in 2015.

incubation period period of time when a virus is spreading in a body but the patient doesn't show signs of infection

The 2014–2016 **epidemic** in West Africa killed more than 11,300 people. More than 28,600 people **contracted** the virus. Aid workers from other countries in Africa, Europe and North America also contracted the virus.

People in the United States worried about Duncan's case. They were afraid of an Ebola outbreak in North America. Health officials found people who came in contact with Duncan. They were **quarantined**. Doctors tested them for Ebola. They had to be cleared by health officials.

Xylo-Mepha
La pantie moderne d'efficacité maxi
Do e exact

Health workers tested people with infrared thermometers. These thermometers can tell if a person has a fever without touching the person's skin.

epidemic outbreak of a disease that affects many people within a particular region
contract become infected with a disease
quarantine isolate something in order to prevent disease from spreading

CHAPTER 2

THE FIRST OUTBREAK

Ebola was first diagnosed in 1976 in the African country of Zaire. Zaire is now known as the Democratic Republic of the Congo.

Patients in Zaire went to a rural hospital in August 1976. They were very ill. They had high fevers, headaches, vomiting and diarrhoea. Their symptoms looked like the flu or malaria. But malaria treatments did not work. The patients got worse. Some started bleeding from their eyes. Others got a rash. Many of them died.

Ebola virus

Medical staff knew something else was wrong. The disease spread through the hospital. Workers gave treatments using glass needles. But they did not clean the needles between patients. Other patients in the hospital fell ill with the disease. It also spread to people outside the hospital.

People who live in rural areas may not have access to advanced medical treatments.

FAST FACT

The Ebola virus was named after the Ebola River in Zaire.

A NEW ILLNESS

Doctors in Zaire had never seen this disease. They needed to identify it. They sent blood samples to scientists in Belgium. On 29 September 1976, researchers found the virus that was making people sick. They sent samples to researchers in the UK and United States. Scientists there did more research. They named the virus *Ebola*.

Meanwhile, patients in Sudan began showing similar symptoms to those of the patients in Zaire. Scientists received samples from these patients. They discovered that the two outbreaks were different types of the Ebola virus. This meant there was more than one form of the disease.

Medical workers tried to prevent even more forms from developing. They did this by trying to contain the disease. They kept sick people away from healthy people. They buried bodies quickly after people died.

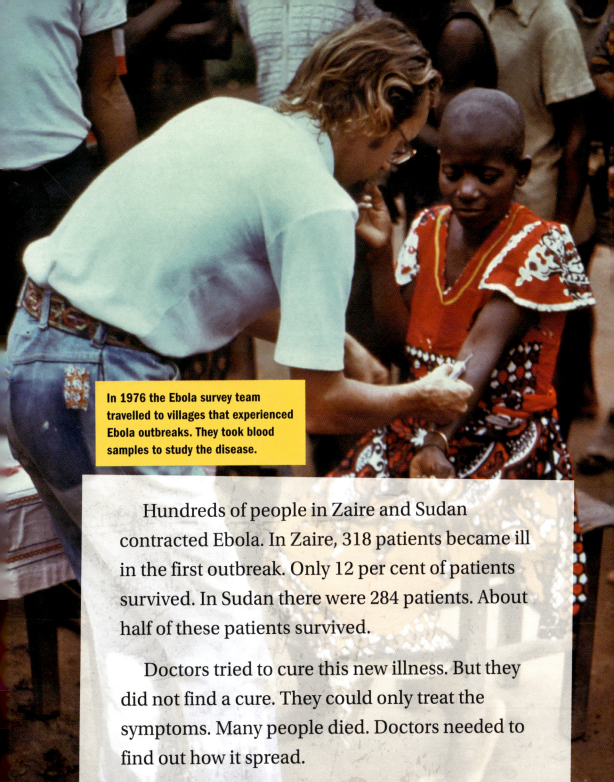

In 1976 the Ebola survey team travelled to villages that experienced Ebola outbreaks. They took blood samples to study the disease.

Hundreds of people in Zaire and Sudan contracted Ebola. In Zaire, 318 patients became ill in the first outbreak. Only 12 per cent of patients survived. In Sudan there were 284 patients. About half of these patients survived.

Doctors tried to cure this new illness. But they did not find a cure. They could only treat the symptoms. Many people died. Doctors needed to find out how it spread.

CHAPTER 3

THE SPREAD OF EBOLA

Before 1994, Ebola was only found in Sudan and the Democratic Republic of the Congo, which was then called Zaire. These outbreaks were in rural areas. They were small and quickly contained. But the virus arrived in other countries in 1994. Doctors learned more about Ebola as it spread across Africa. They learned how the virus spread between people.

14

Ebola spreads through contact with body fluids such as spit, blood and breast milk. Ebola can live for several hours on hard surfaces. These include door handles and tables. People have to regularly clean the rooms of Ebola patients.

Symptoms such as fever, vomiting and diarrhoea usually appear after 8 to 10 days. But sometimes symptoms show up only two days after contact. They can also appear up to three weeks after contact. Patients are only contagious when they show symptoms. People who survive Ebola are resistant to the disease for up to 10 years.

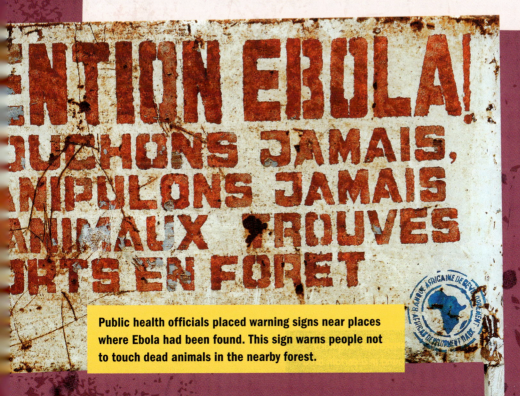

Public health officials placed warning signs near places where Ebola had been found. This sign warns people not to touch dead animals in the nearby forest.

The Ebola virus can live in dead bodies. Many people get infected during burial rituals. Some rituals involve touching the person who died. But this is dangerous if the person died from Ebola.

CONTAINING EBOLA

Most Ebola outbreaks occur in sub-Saharan Africa. They occur most frequently in Sudan, the Democratic Republic of the Congo and Uganda.

Ebola is not **endemic** in countries outside sub-Saharan Africa. The disease has spread to other continents, however, by people travelling from one place to another. Because there is no cure for Ebola, containing the virus is important to stopping future outbreaks.

FAST FACT

Médecins Sans Frontières (MSF) is an aid organization. It is also known as Doctors Without Borders. It helps countries where diseases such as Ebola are endemic. In 2007 MSF workers in Uganda helped to completely contain an Ebola epidemic.

endemic regularly found in a certain area

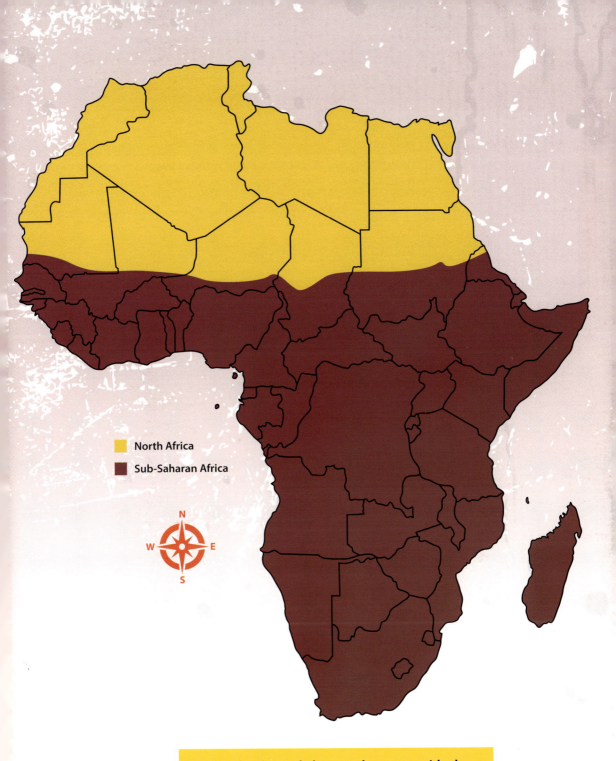

North Africa

Sub-Saharan Africa

N
W E
S

Ebola outbreaks regularly appear in many countries in sub-Saharan Africa. But not all countries in sub-Saharan Africa have experienced outbreaks.

Aid workers contain the virus so that outbreaks stay in small areas. Doctors isolate Ebola patients. They also separate people who may have come into contact with Ebola. Possible Ebola patients are isolated until after the incubation period. Doctors can monitor them for signs of Ebola.

Aid workers attend classes to learn how to treat Ebola patients while keeping the virus contained.

PPE includes special suits that cover workers' entire bodies. Shields cover their faces. They breathe through oxygen tanks. This equipment protects workers. The CDC says that skin should not be exposed. This prevents the spread of the virus. Gowns, gloves, hoods and boots are all thrown away after each use.

Some aid workers from other countries go to areas with Ebola outbreaks. They use personal protective equipment (PPE). PPE rules tell aid workers what type of equipment they need to stay safe. This equipment protects doctors and aid workers from contracting Ebola. PPE also prevents the spread of the illness outside the hospital. If aid workers can contain the virus, outbreaks remain small.

personal protective equipment

CHAPTER 4

THE GLOBAL THREAT

After the first outbreak in 1976, Ebola outbreaks were small. They occurred in rural areas. People were isolated from large cities.

Companies that make medicine did not work on an Ebola **vaccine**. Ebola did not travel very far. Researchers wanted to create vaccines for other diseases first. Countries where Ebola is endemic did not have money to fund vaccine research. Ebola also did not affect many people. But scientists knew that the disease would be hard to contain if it reached a big city.

vaccine   substance made up of dead, weakened or living organisms that is given to a person to protect against a disease

THE 2014 EPIDEMIC

In December 2013, a toddler in Guinea contracted Ebola. Five other people in his village died. Health officials assumed this would be another small outbreak. But the virus did not stay in the rural village.

Ebola spread to the capital of Guinea in 2014. This was the first time Ebola was in an urban area. The disease spread quickly because many people lived close together.

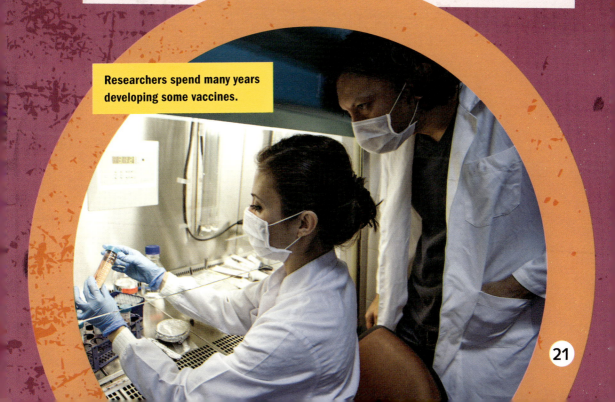

Researchers spend many years developing some vaccines.

By the end of March 2014, there were 49 confirmed cases of Ebola. Twenty-nine people had died. The World Health Organization (WHO) declared an epidemic. Ebola was not contained. Guinea did not have the supplies or hospitals to handle Ebola patients. Doctors in Guinea did not know how to stop the spread of Ebola.

People carried the illness to Liberia and Sierra Leone in July 2014. These countries were not ready to contain the disease either. People did not know how to protect themselves from Ebola. Doctors in these countries were still learning about it.

EBOLA AROUND THE WORLD

People in the United States became worried about Ebola after Duncan arrived. Amber Vinson and Nina Pham treated Duncan. They became the first people to contract Ebola from someone else in the United States. They both survived.

TREATMENTS AND VACCINES

Currently there is no antiviral medication for Ebola. Treatment includes fighting the symptoms. This gives the body time to fight the virus on its own. Doctors use IV fluids that contain **electrolytes**. Ebola can cause dehydration through vomiting and diarrhoea. Fluids and electrolytes return nutrients to the body.

Doctors also use fever reducers and oxygen. Fever reducers keep the patient comfortable. Oxygen helps the patient's body maintain a stable blood pressure. These treatments keep a person's immune system strong.

Vaccine research sped up during the 2014 epidemic. Researchers wanted to stop the spread of the disease. Scientists noticed that people who recovered from Ebola were resistant to it. They used that information to help their research.

electrolyte element such as calcium or sodium that helps the body stay healthy

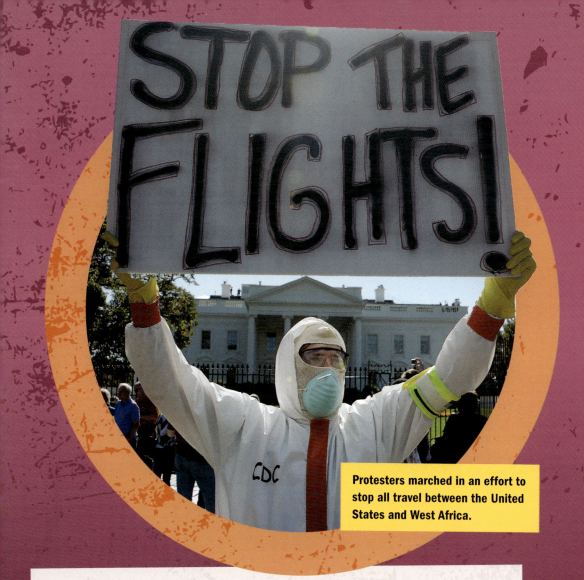

Protesters marched in an effort to stop all travel between the United States and West Africa.

Health officials ordered people who visited Africa to self-quarantine even if they were thousands of kilometres from an outbreak. Government officials proposed travel bans to keep people out of the United States if they had been near Guinea, Liberia or Sierra Leone.

THE SPREAD OF PANIC

People were very afraid of Ebola spreading. In the US, a teacher from Maine went to a conference in Dallas, Texas. It was around 16 kilometres (10 miles) from the hospital where Duncan was treated. After returning from the conference, she was placed on medical leave in case she accidentally came into contact with Ebola. Many people were afraid of being in the same room or on the same plane as someone who had come into contact with Ebola. According to one public health official, the panic about Ebola was "harder to contain than the . . . disease itself".

Some health officials worried that Ebola would turn into a **pandemic** that could not be contained. But these predictions never came true. There were only 10 Ebola cases in the United States in 2014. In 2015, there was only one. Other than Duncan, Vinson, Pham and Spencer, all Ebola patients were purposely brought to the United States to receive treatment. In the UK, nobody caught Ebola from someone else.

pandemic spread of a disease across multiple countries

GLOSSARY

antibody cell that fights off infections

antiviral medication used to treat viruses

contagious spreadable

contract become infected with a disease

dehydrated state of not having enough water

electrolyte element such as calcium or sodium that helps the body stay healthy

endemic regularly found in a certain area

epidemic outbreak of a disease that affects many people within a particular region

incubation period period of time when a virus is spreading in a body but the patient doesn't show signs of infection

intravenous entering the body through veins

isolate keep separate

pandemic spread of a disease across multiple countries

quarantine isolate something in order to prevent disease from spreading

vaccine substance made up of dead, weakened or living organisms that is given to a person to protect against a disease

Researchers used observations to test their theory that bats are a reservoir. Some Ebola patients in the 1976 Sudan outbreak worked in a factory. Bats roosted in the ceiling. People came in contact with bat faeces and spit. People who live near the rainforest also eat bats. They eat fruit and plants that could have come into contact with bat faeces or spit. Scientists believe this is how the virus is spread from animals to humans.

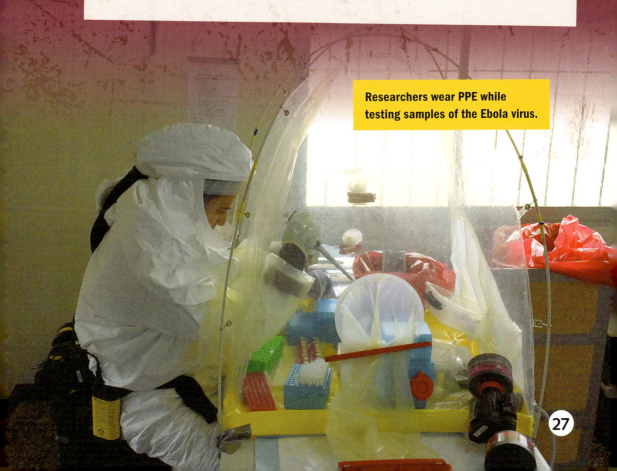

Researchers wear PPE while testing samples of the Ebola virus.

Today doctors are testing experimental vaccines during new Ebola outbreaks. They use a method called "ring vaccination". This means doctors vaccinate people who have come into contact with someone who already has Ebola. Research shows that this vaccination technique helps slow the spread of the virus. Rings of people act like a barrier. The virus does not affect as many people.

Health workers in western and central Africa continue trying to contain Ebola outbreaks. Many people work to improve hospitals, supplies and emergency plans in countries where outbreaks occur. Containing the spread of Ebola is crucial to avoiding a pandemic.

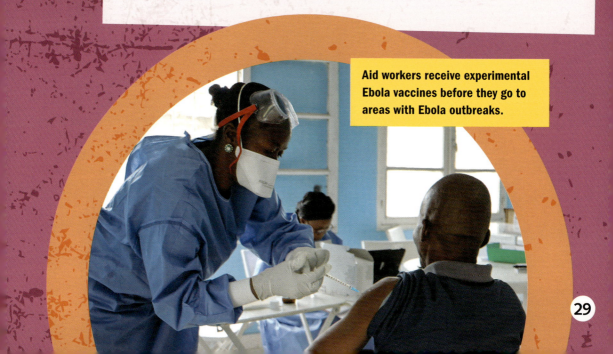

Aid workers receive experimental Ebola vaccines before they go to areas with Ebola outbreaks.

Today doctors are testing experimental vaccines during new Ebola outbreaks. They use a method called "ring vaccination". This means doctors vaccinate people who have come into contact with someone who already has Ebola. Research shows that this vaccination technique helps slow the spread of the virus. Rings of people act like a barrier. The virus does not affect as many people.

Health workers in western and central Africa continue trying to contain Ebola outbreaks. Many people work to improve hospitals, supplies and emergency plans in countries where outbreaks occur. Containing the spread of Ebola is crucial to avoiding a pandemic.

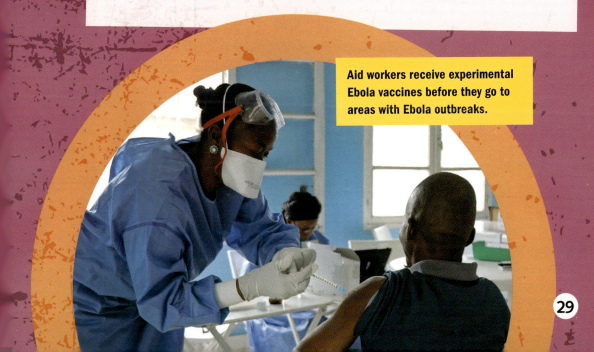

Aid workers receive experimental Ebola vaccines before they go to areas with Ebola outbreaks.

GLOSSARY

antibody cell that fights off infections

antiviral medication used to treat viruses

contagious spreadable

contract become infected with a disease

dehydrated state of not having enough water

electrolyte element such as calcium or sodium that helps the body stay healthy

endemic regularly found in a certain area

epidemic outbreak of a disease that affects many people within a particular region

incubation period period of time when a virus is spreading in a body but the patient doesn't show signs of infection

intravenous entering the body through veins

isolate keep separate

pandemic spread of a disease across multiple countries

quarantine isolate something in order to prevent disease from spreading

vaccine substance made up of dead, weakened or living organisms that is given to a person to protect against a disease

FIND OUT MORE

BOOKS

Can You Survive a Virus Outbreak?: An Interactive Doomsday Adventure, Matt Doeden (Raintree, 2015)

Health and Disease: From Birth to Old Age (Your Body for Life), Louise Spilsbury (Raintree, 2013)

Promoting Health, Preventing Disease (The Environment Challenge), Rebecca Vickers (Raintree, 2012)

You Wouldn't Want to Live Without Vaccinations! Anne Rooney (Franklin Watts, 2015)

WEBSITES

www.bbc.co.uk/newsround/28952811
Learn more about Ebola.

www.dkfindout.com/uk/human-body/body-defences/germs-and-disease
Find out more about germs and disease.

INDEX